How to Make Money Online: The Ultimate Money Making Playbook for Success

Author: Adella Pasos

Are you interested in making money online? The ultimate money making playbook for success is your new best friend in business. This comprehensive strategy guide will reveal to you the most popular methods of making money online today. Whether you are a solo entrepreneur, a small startup or a large enterprise corporation, you will benefit from the strategies in this book. Learn simple, yet effective cash producing monetization strategies that are used by companies across the globe.

Finally, the book contains advice that you can believe in. All strategies are being actively used and are easy to set up. So, if you're seeking to generate passive income online or build a million dollar business with more than one revenue source, this is the book you need today.

How to Make Money Online: The Ultimate Money Making Playbook for Success

Published by Adella Pasos

Copyright © 2020 www.adellapasos.com

All rights reserved. No part of this book, including interior design, cover design, and icons may be reproduced or transmitted in any form, by any means (electronic, photocopying, recording or otherwise) without the prior written permission of the author, except for the inclusion of brief quotations in a review.

This book also uses affiliate links and does earn a commission from certain links. This does not affect your purchases or the price you may pay. We are independently owned and opinions expressed on this professional website are that of our own.

Table of Contents

Introduction: About This Book

Chapter 1: Promoting & Selling Affiliate Products

This chapter discusses how to earn money by promoting other brand's products or services. You could start earning an affiliate income in only a few hours.

Chapter 2: Sell Branded Merchandise

Learn how to earn royalties from selling your own branded merchandise. This chapter covers print on demand opportunities that are low cost to start up.

Chapter 3: Sell Digital Downloads

Digital products offer a high profit margin and are easy to deliver. Learn how to earn money from selling digital downloads for instant cash flow.

Chapter 4: Sell Sponsorships & Ads

If you've built a website online, own a youtube, a social media page or you are hosting online events that are highly trafficked, you can easily turn them into cash producing assets by selling sponsorships.

Chapter 5: Sell Services

Learn how to capitalize on the skills you already have or by reselling the skills and services of others. Customers are waiting to buy these kinds of services online.

Table of Contents Continued...

Chapter 6: Sell Products

If you are interested in manufacturing your own products, launching a new brand online or just drop shipping other people's products online, then this chapter is for you.

Chapter 7: Start an Online Marketplace

The fastest way to acquire and keep customers is to launch an online marketplace. Choose from B2B or B2C and collect revenue on every item sold or purchased at your online shop.

Chapter 8: Sell Memberships & Subscriptions

What can you offer to your customers that they would be willing to pay for or gain access to? This chapter reveals how to make automated money each month from selling memberships and subscriptions.

Chapter 9: Money Making Resources

This chapter includes a list of impressive resources that will help you make money online today.

Appendix: Frequently Asked Questions

This is a great spot to check out the most common questions people have about other ways to make money and benefits of online business.

Introduction: About This E-Book

Hello! and thanks for downloading this awesome book. Throughout the course of this book you will learn how to profit from money making strategies. I wrote this book for you to truly see that your business can succeed with the help of a great strategy.

The strategies that I've listed in the book will explain how you can get paid from various opportunities online, as well as how to get started. Entrepreneurs, start-ups, and even large fortune 500 companies are using the same strategies to gain millions of dollars. So, where's your piece of the pie? Who doesn't love a fast track to success?

Who am I?

I am an International Business Coach and Marketing Strategist who has shared my passion for growing brands from the ground up. I've worked with startups, small businesses, global corporations and entertainment talent that recognize the value of marketing. I give my clients the ability to sell more by preparing them with the right strategies in social media, mobile, merchandising, and events. Providing simple solutions to complex challenges, I've placed all that I know into these books.

Now, it's time for you to apply the knowledge, and get out there and put your game face on!

Cheers to your success,

Adella Pasos

Chapter 1: Promoting & Selling Affiliate Products

For those of you who have never heard of "affiliate products and services", plain and simple, there are companies who create a marketing agreement with you. They expect you to promote their products in order to generate a sale. Once you generate that sale they pay you a commission for it. The more people you refer that actually make a purchase, the bigger your paycheck will be.

How can an entrepreneur use this strategy?

Selling affiliate products and services allows you to have the freedom to work full-time or part-time. It's virtually free and can be done quickly through an online registration process. Being an affiliate doesn't require any expertise or special product knowledge. You don't even have to handle customers or complaints! **Earn passive income and be your own boss!**

How can an organization use this strategy?

Setting up an affiliate marketing program is a huge revenue driver for any business. It gives you the opportunity to get your products and services in front of hundreds of thousands of people very quickly, and allows you to only pay for performance. Tracking the success of a program is relatively simple and can result in a **lower cost per acquisition** than most traditional forms of marketing and advertising.

How can an entrepreneur get paid?

Many people starting out choose to use an inbound lead generation strategy that consist of creating videos, writing blog posts and articles, webinars, email blasts, buy ads, and promoting through social media and events. **Your promotional options are endless.**

First, select a product or service that you feel comfortable selling. Once you sign up with an affiliate program, they will give you a tool kit complete with promotional banners and a referral link connected to your account & customized just for you to get paid. **You don't have to worry about shipping any product or customer service.** Your only job is to promote & refer, to get paid! Commissions are usually given as a percentage of the product or service's retail price.

How can an organization get paid?

Once your affiliate program is set up and all links and sales can be tracked, you now have to find people who are willing to promote your brand, in exchange for a commission. **You can't and won't get paid until an affiliate actually generates a sale.** Be very strategic about the affiliate approval process, not all affiliates may be able to send you guaranteed sales.

Often, organizations choose to disburse their payouts 45 days after the sale is actually confirmed. You'll need to work with a professional affiliate program company to help you set up the terms of your agreements.

How can I get started?

For brands or for entrepreneurs, you can choose from a variety of products or services to sell and promote from these websites below. However, most large organizations will have an affiliate program already setup. If you are interested in selling your favorite brand or a company's products or services in a specialty niche, just reach out to that company directly and find out if they are accepting affiliates.

- Pepper Jam
- ShareaSale
- Amazon Associates
- CJ Affiliate
- Rakuten Marketing
- Flex Offers
- Click Bank
- eBay Partner Network

- Walmart Affiliates
- Target Affiliates
- JVZoo
- CJ Affiliate
- AvantLink
- PeerFly
- ReviMedia
- Maxbounty

Pick products that you would like to promote or that aligns with your niche. Begin to promote the products online via banner ads, text ads, video review, your blog, or even offline with flyers, by word of mouth, or any way you choose!

PRO TIP: It's really helpful to generate a list of people who may be interested in special offers, or helpful content. Then you can email those people your affiliate product recommendations. This way they are more likely to buy. The brand will take care of the product or service fulfillment and you rake in the cash!

Chapter 2: Sell Branded Merchandise

Selling branded merchandise can be a great way to add revenue and even grow a following if you are an independent entrepreneur. Regardless of if you are a band, a sports team, a model, or a tech company, there are people who can't wait to wear your logo or custom designs on their t-shirts, hats, cell phone cases and more!

How can an entrepreneur use this strategy?

Even if you have or haven't yet created a brand, you can still use this strategy to make money online. There are companies who will allow you to create and sell your own custom designed products online with a print-on-demand drop shipping option. They will ship the products and deal with returns and customer service. Some companies will even provide you a free storefront. **You just design, sell and promote**. Another great way to make passive income.

How can an organization use this strategy?

Using this strategy to make money allows you to strengthen brand loyalty. Often organizations will set up an online store to sell everyday items that are branded with their logo or match the brand's style. They sell t-shirts, hats, pens, notebooks, drinkware, bags, gifts, tech items and more.

The people who will buy this merchandise are usually those who want to show their pride in your brand or they need a gift for friends and family members who support your brand.

How can I get started?

For brands, you need to find a reliable provider to source branded products from. You may choose to drop. ship or just buy in bulk and store the products in your own warehouse for fulfillment.

For independent entrepreneurs, you can work with any of these companies listed below to set up an online print on demand shop. Some of them will pay you a percentage commission on the total amount of products sold, others will give you a dollar amount based on the sale price of the item.

- Zazzle
- CustomInk
- Cafepress
- Teelaunch
- Spreadshirt
- Teespring
- Customcat
- Jet Print
- SPOD
- Redbubble
- Threadless
- Printful

Remember, for these suppliers, there is no upfront cost for the products you sell. No stock to hold. You never need to worry about having space for stock, or paying warehouse fees. Also, usually you can sell as many different products as you'd like. No need to worry about manufacturing products in advance or even fulfillment costs.

Some of them will provide a free or upgraded eCommerce platform for you to sell on their website. However, if they don't you can also list the same products on your own website. They will still be shipped directly to your customers, on-demand.

Chapter 3: Sell Digital Downloads

Selling digital downloads allow you to make money on-demand with products you only need to create one time. Digital products have a much higher profit margin and are easier to deliver. **Examples of top selling digital products are:** templates, worksheets, forms, photography, music and beats, research pdf, e-books, stock video footage, and courses.

How can an entrepreneur use this strategy?

If you've decided to sell digital products, you'll need to either set up a store online where customers can easily download these products from you. Or, there are many platforms that will provide a free place for you to sell your digital products, but they will take a small percentage of each item you sell. *Easy to set up, promote and generate passive income.*

How can an organization use this strategy?

An organization can use this strategy to up-sell, down-sell, or cross-sell a low cost and extremely profitable digitally delivered item to their current customers or prospects. You may also decide to simply sell a subscription to access all of your digital items each month for recurring revenue. Remember digital products last forever and can never go "out of stock". So, your company has unlimited potential to sell complimentary items that are digital and *generate even more revenue.*

How can I get started?

For brands, you can create an addition to your website, like a shop or online marketplace for people to buy these digital products. You will need to hire someone internally to create the products and manage the store, or you can outsource these tasks through a company like Fiverr.

For independent entrepreneurs, you can work with any of these companies listed below to set up an online store to sell digital products. Some of them will pay you a percentage commission on the total amount of products sold, others will give you a dollar amount based on the sale price of the item.

- Gumroad Selz
- Payhip
- Thinkific
- Fast Spring
- Simple Goods

- SendOwl
- FetchApp
- DPD (Digital Product Delivery)
- e-Junkie
- Payloadz
- Envato Market

Remember, for these suppliers, there is no upfront cost for the products you sell. Some of them will provide a free or upgraded eCommerce platform for you to sell on their website. However, if they don't you can always list your digital products on your own website. Your customers can still get what they need and download directly from you.

Chapter 4: Sell Sponsorships & Ads

If your website, app, social media account, or events draw in a bunch of traffic, you may be able to find sponsors. Sponsors are brands that will pay you in exchange for marketing or exposure on your networks. Often they will pay to be mentioned on your video content, in your podcast, or at your events / webinars.

They will also buy ad space on your website, in your email blasts or on blog posts, just because your audience is among their target groups of people they are interested in selling to.

How can an entrepreneur use this strategy?

If you've decided to sell sponsorships, the first thing you'll need to do is assess your eligibility to sell. Make sure you are able to document and explain to a potential sponsor your audience's demographics, your website's traffic stats, how many people their ads will reach, how many people are on your email list, how many views you get on your videos, and what your engagement looks like on your content. **The higher these numbers, the more money you are able to ask for and receive.**

How can an organization use this strategy?

If an organization is already throwing annual award ceremonies, golf outings, or educational business events? Small and large companies alike will pay you to have their brand recognized or mentioned at your events or in your email blasts. Get a sponsorship package PDF designed with 99designs and start selling to **increase your revenue and overall return** on these events and activities that are already taking place.

How can I get started?

If you want to sell ads on media assets (website, blog, youtube, email list, etc) that you own. Here is a list of companies who can help you monetize.

- Google Adsense
- OpenX
- AdPushUp
- Conversant Media
- Infolinks
- LiveIntent
- Youtube Partner
- Facebook Audience Network

- Centro
- BuySell Ads
- Vibrant Media
- Amobee
- AdMedia
- VigLink
- Virool
- BrightCove

If you want to sell sponsorships for your webinars, online or physical events, here's a list of websites that can help.

- Eventbrite
- Sponsor Pitch
- Izea
- BiddingOwl

- Hookit
- SplashThat
- myevent
- Famebit

Chapter 5: Sell Services

Selling services is a great way to make money online. Through e-commerce, the fulfillment and delivery of services is now easier than ever before. Capitalize on the skills you already have or even re-sell the skills and services of others to make even more money.

How can an entrepreneur use this strategy?

Whether you want to sell to other companies or to consumers, selling services means selling yourself, your competencies, you or your team's expertise and the value you bring to your target market. To implement this strategy, make a plan of services you want to sell, write up a description for each and set the prices you want to charge. Once complete, set up an online shop, enter the information and begin to promote to generate sales.

How can an organization use this strategy?

There are many organizations today, who are already selling services and are looking to add more. And, there are those who only sell products, but would like to begin selling services, too! Whichever position you are in, your first step is to generate a list of potential services you can quickly get done and deliver online. Put some thought into what services could add additional value to the products or services your customers are currently buying from you. Come up with a list of services that are low-cost and highly profitable to deliver.

70 Services You Can Start Selling Today

The service sector has long outperformed any other area of commerce in the economy. Here's a list of service you can easily start start selling or add on to your business today:

1. cloud hosting services
2. managed IT services
3. restoration services
4. writing services
5. marketing / creative / lead generation services
6. backup services
7. protection services
8. insurance services
9. consulting services
10. design services
11. training / tutoring services
12. assistant services
13. installation services
14. planning services
15. reporting services
16. search services
17. removal services
18. cleaning and repair services

15. tour services
16. photography / videography services
17. monitoring services
18. matching services
19. identification check services
20. recording and documentation services
21. filing / processing services
22. scanning services
23. development / production services
24. interpretation services
25. transportation services
26. assessment services
27. management services
28. evaluation services
29. building services
30. investment services
31. delivery services
32. preservation services
33. auditing services
34. preparation services
35. maintenance services
36. investigation services
37. financial management services
38. testing services
39. shopping services
40. research services
41. sales services
42. storage services

43. fulfillment services
44. translation services
45. advisory / counseling services
46. distribution services
47. conversion services
48. mixing / mastering services
49. packaging or labeling services
50. compilation or reproduction services
51. security services
52. guard services
53. collection services
54. treatment services
55. duplication services
56. response services
57. relocation services
58. shipping services
59. support services
60. adjustment / alteration services
61. project management services
62. surveying services
63. mapping services
64. supervisory services
65. budgeting services
66. administration services
67. printing services
68. sorting services
69. disposal services
70. rental services

Chapter 6: Sell Products

If you are interested in manufacturing your own products, launching a new brand online or just drop shipping other people's products online you can make big money doing so.

Entrepreneurs and Organizations Both Use This Strategy

If you want to sell products online, you have three options to start.

Option 1: Manufacture and sell your own products online.

Option 2: Find, source, buy wholesale and stock products in your own warehouse to sell online.

Option 3: Signup for a drop ship program to sell other people's products (without holding physical inventory). Depending on the product's level of demand and niche you've selected. You can rake in pretty good money selling physical products online.

Steps to Get Started

- Decide on a niche
- Do research on the types of products in demand
- Find out the cost to manufacture, buy wholesale or dropship
- Decide on a strategy and choose a vendor
- Incorporate your business (if not already done)
- Setup a website or list your products in an online marketplace
- Market and promote your product listings
- Accept payment for products
- Ship, deliver or make sure product is successfully fulfilled
- Ask customers for reviews after received

Chapter 7: Start an Online Marketplace

Starting an online marketplace is a great way to bring people together to buy and sell, but also to generate income. There are a lot of merchants who have items they don't have a use for anymore , are storing extra inventory or would simply like more sales. Your job is to connect them to potential buyers and you'll **get paid** to do it.

Entrepreneurs and Organizations Both Use This Strategy

Building a successful marketplace is not always easy, but you can quickly recoup your startup costs by charging fees such as: listing fees, transaction fees (by volume sold), commissions, subscription fees, lead generation fees, advertising fees, setup fees, processing fees and more. This strategy allows you to easily make money online as long as the business processes are automated.

Steps to Get Started

- Research your target market
- Choose a business model **(B2B or B2C)**
- Plan the marketplace revenue model
- Decide on a strategy and choose a vendor
- Outline essential website features
- <u>Incorporate your business</u> **(if not already done)**
- <u>Create your branding & logo</u>
- <u>Buy</u> a domain & setup a website
- <u>Choose a website payment solution provider</u>
- Assemble a team to build out your platform
- Launch your platform
- Start marketing and promoting for sellers to join
- Collect fees on every item they sell

Chapter 8: Sell Memberships & Subscriptions

If you are interested in making consistent, passive income online, selling memberships or subscriptions to a product or service will work for you. Members of your website will pay for things like special access to exclusive video content, free or reduced fees, special discounts from brands, discounts on your conferences, the ability to get expedited shipping on all products, unlimited downloads every month, additional bonus features, priority seating, etc.

Entrepreneurs and Organizations Both Use This Strategy

If you've been spending time growing an audience, you know that generating revenue and profits out of them is essential for you to continue business operations. It's time to start thinking about what you want to offer to your customers that they would be willing to pay for or gain priority access to?

Once you decide on your membership or subscription service offerings. Pick a place where they can easily transact with you online to subscribe or become a new member. **People are currently paying for these type of benefits:**

- Monthly exclusive seminars
- Private facebook groups
- Members only deals or coupons
- Member-only Forums
- Community Exclusive Discounts
- Expertise at your fingertips
- Uninterrupted support

- Premium templates
- On-demand advice
- Upgraded security or protection services
- Live events / live access
- Special tutorials & step-by-step guides
- Access to new content

How can I get started?

You can easily implement a payment portal to accept subscription and membership sign ups into your own website, by <u>hiring a web developer</u>. Communicate the price and description of what you are selling and ensure the developer can update your website to accept those kinds of payments and deliver the goods.

If you don't already have a website, you can work with one of these companies who will host your membership or subscription online.

- Paypal Payments Pro
- ChargeBee
- Subhub
- aMember
- Sellfy

- Personify
- Memberful
- Wishlist Member
- Podia
- SendOwl

Chapter 9: Money Making Resources

Email Marketing - Aweber

The world's best email marketing software for business newsletters and auto-responders! Create emails with style and get more messages delivered fast! Create professional and powerful email marketing today.

Get a Free Trial of Aweber for Email Marketing

Web Hosting - Bluehost

I highly recommend using Bluehost for your website. They have an incredibly easy to use 1-click automatic word press installation and amazing customer service. The link below gets you a special discount off the regular price!

Get a 30 Day Money Back Guarantee for a New Website

Business Incorporation - MyCorporation

Everything you need to start, maintain and protect your business. Easily form a corporation or Limited Liability Company in no time. Learn which entity is best for your business!

Legally Incorporate Your Business Today

Website Analytics & SEO - SEMRush

The world's best digital marketing tool that helps you with marketing direction and drives sales through insights. With this tool, you get total visibility on any competitors' marketing strategy.

Get a Free Trial of SEMRush

Marketing Designers - 99Designs

I highly recommend using 99designs if you need a logo, online marketing materials, pdfs, press kits, labels, email marketing, just about anything designed.

Launch a free account and start a project with 99designs

Business Supply Purchases - Amazon Business

Create a free Amazon Business account to save time and money on business purchases with competitive B2B prices and discounts. Satisfy your sourcing requirements and get Tax-exempt purchasing.

Get Discounted Supplies with Amazon for Business

Appendix: "Frequently Asked Questions"

Q: How can I sell other people's products, without affiliate marketing?

A: You can go to google and search for white label products, or you can start a drop shop model business.

Q: Will affiliate marketing cost me any money?

A: Yes and no. If you are looking to generate fast traffic to the brand's or your own offers, you will need to invest in paid traffic. If you already have a list of prospects or buyers who may be interested, the only cost is your time to email them your product recommendations. You can always use organic traffic to generate sales as well. Those are usually not low cost methods.

Q: Can I work as a freelancer online? What places can I list my services to sell?

A: You can list them on your own website, or websites like Upwork, Fiverr, Freelancer, Guru, or TaskRabbit.

Q: Should I hire someone to start selling?

A: If you want to start generating revenue or income as soon as possible, I would recommend that you personally start selling or you set up a system that sells for you. Do that until you get enough stable cash flow to pay employees.

Q: How can I get digital products created to sell online?

A: You can either hire someone to create them, on a marketplace like Upwork or Fiverr. These website's are filled with freelancers who are willing to design or create content for you.

You can create them yourself, or you can buy 'done for you plr' content online. This is content that is ready to be sold and you own the rights to re-publish or convert them into any other media type and sell online.

Q: Do I need to register an actual business before I can become an affiliate marketer?

A: Not necessarily, some affiliate networks and companies will approve you as long as you have an EIN tax number to verify that you are only a sole proprietor. However, many of them prefer that you have incorporated under an LLC, at least to start.

About the Author

MARKETING EXPERT | BRAND STRATEGIST | BUSINESS COACH | TV HOST

This Business Coach and Marketing Expert has shared her passion for growing brands from the ground up. She's worked with Startups, Small Businesses, Fortune 500 Corporations and entertainment talent that recognize the value of marketing. She gives her clients the ability to access their niche market via online, social media, mobile, merchandising, and events.

The What's Your Game Plan Show features free expert advice and growth strategies for Business Owners and Executives across the globe.

Access thousands of FREE Tips, Trends and Tools to Move Your Business Forward! Contact the author:

AdellaPasos.com
Subscribe to Business Strategy TV Youtube

www.ingramcontent.com/pod-product-compliance
Lightning Source LLC
Chambersburg PA
CBHW081710220526
45466CB00009B/2939